These are adding to the greenhouse effect – the over-heating of the Earth's atmosphere. Deforestation is a particular problem in the forests of the less-developed countries, like Brazil, Malaysia and the Philippines.

Pollution of the air by harmful gases from factories, power stations and vehicles causes **acid rain** (see page 10). This attacks trees and plants, leaving them unhealthy or even killing them. Acid rain is a particular problem in the forests of industrialized countries like Canada, West Germany and Sweden.

We must all share the blame. For example, although less-developed countries do most of the deforestation today, the richer countries did the same in the past. Developed countries also lend money to the poor countries for projects that encourage deforestation, and they buy up the timber as it is cut down. In addition, developed countries are responsible for producing most of the gases that cause acid rain.

Both problems – deforestation and acid rain – affect everyone. If we allow our planet to warm up and our forests to go on disappearing, then we and our children will have to suffer the disastrous results of a changing climate. Thousands of kinds of animals and plants will be lost for ever. The disappearing forests are a shared problem for all of humankind to face.

WHY DO PEOPLE DESTROY THE FORESTS?

● To obtain timber for buildings, tools, carvings and other wooden objects.
● For firewood used in cooking, heating and factory processes.
● To clear the ground for roads, factories, houses and farmland (see page 26).
● To obtain valuable minerals from the ground by mining (see page 29).
● In some cases, simply to stake a claim to the land.

SHRINKING GREEN BAND

There are many kinds of forests around the world. The types of trees and plants, and the animals that live among them, depend on the effects of temperature, rainfall and other factors of the **climate**. Biologists recognize several main kinds of forests.

Tropical rainforests stretch across the world on either side of the equator, from Central and South America, through western Africa, right across southern Asia to northern Australia. They cover about one-sixteenth of the Earth's surface. A tropical rainforest needs at least 200 centimetres of rainfall each year – that is why it is called a "rain"-forest. In such warm, wet places, the trees are mainly broad-leaved, but they keep their leaves all year round; they are called evergreens.

Temperate forests grow mainly north of the equator; few grow in the south. They consist mostly of oaks, beeches, maples and other broad-leaved trees that lose their leaves in winter; they are called deciduous trees.

LOST FORESTS

- Ivory Coast – 14 million hectares lost in 25 years.
- Malaysia – the peninsular forests are almost all gone.
- Congo – 68% of the forest is to be cut for logging.
- Nigeria – complete deforestation by 2000.
- Guinea – 30% of its forest lost by 2000.
- Madagascar – 30% of forest lost by 2000.

FOREST DESTRUCTION

The map opposite shows the main areas of forest and forest destruction. The rainforest of Central America and the Amazon (inset) is being destroyed at the rate of about 25,000 square kilometres a year.

TROPICAL RAINFORESTS
Tropical forests once covered a large part of the tropics, but many are now under threat.

BROAD-LEAVED FORESTS
Temperate forests mostly grow north of the equator as there is little suitable land in the south.

CONIFEROUS FORESTS
Conifers are found mostly in the northern hemisphere as far north as the Arctic tundra.

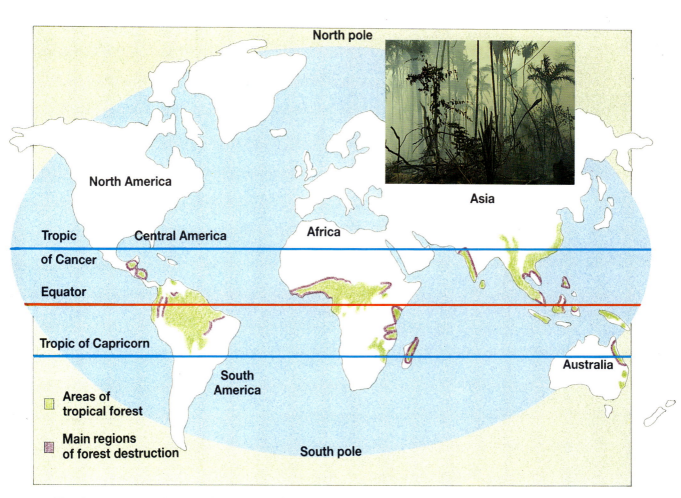

North pole

North America

Asia

Tropic
of Cancer
Central America
Africa

Equator

Tropic of Capricorn

Areas of
tropical forest

Main regions
of forest destruction

South
America

Australia

South pole

Further north still are the boreal forests. Here most of the trees are conifers such as firs, pines and spruces. They too are evergreen, and they keep their needle-shaped leaves during the long, snowy winters.

Tropical rainforests are disappearing very fast. Some scientists believe that the rainforests cover only half the area they once did. We are losing at least 100,000 square kilometres each year, which is three-quarters the area of England or of the US state of New York (see page 20). An even vaster area, the size of Britain or Colorado in the USA, is damaged but not destroyed, and loses many of its plants and animals.

The temperate forests are being cut down, too. In the USA, an area the size of 20,000 soccer pitches disappears each year. These are mostly ancient temperate forests near the north-west coast and Alaska. It will take at least 100 years, and probably nearer 400, for these forests to grow back again.

?

REPLANTING THE FORESTS?

In Canada, only three new trees are planted for every 10 that are cut down. In other regions, some scientists argue that the felling of forests is "in balance". Trees are replanted at the same rate as they are chopped down.

ACID RAIN

Acid rain and air pollution are killing millions of trees in the deciduous and coniferous forests (see page 8). Chemicals such as sulphur dioxide and nitrogen oxides are present in smoke from power stations that burn coal, oil and gas, and in exhaust fumes from cars and trucks. In the atmosphere, the chemicals combine with water to produce acid rain. The acid rain falls on to the land and attacks trees and other plants, leaving them unhealthy. Strong acid rain kills trees. It also harms animals, including humans.

THE TOLL OF ACID RAIN

● Each year in the USA, air pollution is thought to cause up to 50,000 deaths.

● Air pollution is particularly bad in and around big cities. In some, like Mexico City, there are few limits on what vehicles, power stations and factories release into the atmosphere. Such places are particularly unsafe. The air in Mexico City can give people sore throats within minutes of going outdoors.

● Polluted air is particularly bad for people with chest complaints. Deaths in Athens, Greece, are six times more common on heavily polluted days than on days when there is little pollution.

MEXICO CITY
A thick fog covers Mexico city for much of the time. Sometimes the smog is so dense that the city cannot be seen from the air.

ACID RAIN FROM AFAR

The gases that cause acid rain are blown by the wind. Acid rain that falls in Scandinavia comes from gases produced by factories and power stations in the surrounding industrialized countries (see below).

ACID-KILLED FORESTS

Many coniferous forests in Scandinavia, Czechoslovakia (shown right) and Canada are being killed by acid rain.

TOO LITTLE TOO LATE

Widespread ill-health of forests in Western Europe led to the first government agreements to cut down sulphur dioxide and nitrogen oxide fumes from power stations, in the mid-1980s. The cuts are 57% of sulphur dioxide by the year 2003, and 70% of nitrogen oxides by 1998. But scientists have described this as "too little, too late". European forests continue to suffer badly from acid rain.

A recent survey by the Worldwatch Institute shows that more than one-fifth of the world's population now breathes air that is polluted beyond international safety limits. Most of the polluting chemicals contribute to acid rain. Air loaded with the chemicals drifts away from cities and industrial areas to the countryside. It attacks trees in two ways. It damages their leaves directly, harming the tiny holes in the leaf's skin, which are used in transpiration to control its water content (see page 22). Or, as acid rain, the chemicals seep into the soil and attack the roots of the trees. The roots are damaged because too much of the substance aluminium is taken up and this prevents the roots from absorbing the correct **nutrients**.

Damage to trees as a result of acid rain has happened in many parts of the world. Scandinavian countries noticed their dying forests and polluted lakes in the 1960s, which they blamed on acid rain from British industries. Damage in Canadian forests has been blamed on industries in the USA.

LIFE IN RAINFORESTS

Famous creatures such as the mountain gorilla, the tiger and the orang-utan live in the rainforests. So do the beautiful birds of paradise and brightly-coloured parrots. Exotic orchids and rare butterflies add colour to the scene. However, these animals and plants are only a tiny fraction of the rainforest inhabitants.

Animals and plants can be grouped into species, and the species are grouped into families. The tiger, for example, is a species of the cat family. The date palm is a species of the palm-tree family. This method of grouping, or classification, helps scientists to describe life on Earth. The species is the basic "unit" in the natural world. Individuals in one species can breed together, or reproduce, to create more of their kind. They cannot breed with members of another species.

THE AMAZING DIVERSITY

● From 10 hectares of Indonesian rainforest (an area the size of about 12 soccer pitches), a scientist found no fewer than 700 species of tree. This is about the same as the number of tree species found in the whole of North America.
● The rainforests of the small country of Panama have as many plant species as the whole of Europe.
● From a single tree in the rainforest of Peru, the famous American biologist Professor Edward Wilson found 43 species of ants – the same number as in the whole of Britain.

ANIMALS UNDER THREAT

The Trinidad leaf frog (right) is one of the many small vertebrates under threat because of loss of its forest home.

Orang-utans (above) live in the forests of Borneo. They mostly eat fruit but will also feed on leaves and seeds. They too are in danger of extinction.

HOT LIPS

The hot lips plant (shown left) is found in the understorey of the tropical rainforests of Trinidad. The tiny yellow flower lies in the centre of two modified leaves called bracts.

There are millions of species in the rainforests. Scientists have described about 1,400,000 (1.4 million) species so far on Earth. But there are many, many more to be discovered. Every time scientists study a new area of rainforest, they find new species that they did not know about before. Most are new insects and plants. Scientists have estimated that there are at least 4 million species on our planet, and possibly as many as 30 million. Never before in the history of the world have there been as many species as there are today. We know this from the evidence of fossils, which are the remains of past species preserved in the rocks. Many millions of years of **evolution** (the change of animals and plants over time to produce new species) have gone into developing so many different kinds of animals and plants.

The majority of species are found in two particular areas or habitats: tropical rainforests and coral reefs. Of these two, the tropical rainforests are the main source of new forms of life. More than half of the species on Earth live in them.

LIFE UNDER THREAT

Recently, a ridge of land was cleared of trees in the rainforest of Peru. This is one of the very few places where scientists have been able to study the forest in detail and describe all the species. They found 90 kinds of plants which grew only in that locality. Now the forest is gone, and those species are lost for ever – they have become **extinct**.

This is very depressing when we consider that only about 1 in 100 rainforest plants has been tested for use in medicine. So far such tests on plants have shown

WHAT THEY SAY

"Virtually all ecologists, and I include myself among them, would argue that every species extinction [every animal or plant that dies out] diminishes humanity."
Professor Edward Wilson, in an article in Scientific American in 1989.

SPECIES IN DANGER

MAHOGANY TREE
Wood from the mahogany tree was used to make beautiful furniture. So many trees have been felled that the mahogany now faces extinction.

WOOLLY SPIDER MONKEY
The woolly spider monkey lives in the Brazilian coastal forest. Deforestation has destroyed its home and this monkey is in danger of disappearing.

what we might be losing. One in every four medicines used by doctors today contains substances discovered in rainforest plants.

We are losing many species with every small patch of forest destroyed. Professor Edward Wilson, an expert on rainforests, has calculated that tropical deforestation could be making up to 6000 species extinct every year – that is, one species every two hours! It may be happening even faster than this. In his sums, Professor Wilson assumes that there are only two million species of plants and animals in the tropical rainforests. There are almost certainly many more.

It is not just the undiscovered species that are under threat. Thousands of plants and animals, including many well-known favourites, are in danger of disappearing. Each orang-utan needs several square kilometres of rainforest to provide shelter and food. Deforestation in Sumatra and Borneo means that suitable forest is shrinking rapidly.

LOST HABITATS – LOST LIVES

"Extinctions of plant and animal species will increase dramatically. Hundreds of thousands of species – perhaps as many as 20% of all species on earth – will be … lost as their habitats vanish, especially rainforests."
Global 2000 Report

CLOUDED LEOPARD
The clouded leopard is a very good climber. It feeds mainly on monkeys, squirrels and birds. Its forest home is being destroyed and it is being hunted for its beautiful skin. Soon it will be just one of many endangered species.

PYGMY CHIMP
The pygmy chimp lives in the African rainforest. So much of its natural habitat has been destroyed that it is now an endangered species.

RAFFLESIA
Rafflesia, a parasite, takes all its food from other plants. The only visible part is its huge flower.

RAINFORESTS

From an aircraft, the rainforest looks like an impenetrable green carpet, but walking through the trees can actually be quite easy. The thick foliage forms a "roof" many metres up. This tangle of branches, leaves, twigs, flowers and fruits lets little light filter through, so that few plants can survive in the gloom on the forest floor below. Seen from the side, a typical rainforest has three horizontal "layers", made by trees and plants that grow to different heights. The top layer, the canopy, is about 30-40 metres from the ground, and this is where most animals live.

Despite the great variety of life, the soil of a rainforest is usually poor in quality. Unlike the temperate forests, which often have thick, rich soils, there are few nutrients to feed the growing plants in rainforest soils. This means if you clear the trees and grow crops, the harvest will only last about two or three years. After this, the goodness of the soil will be exhausted, and the soil may be washed away by the heavy rain. To allow nutrients to build up again, it may be necessary to leave the soils for as long as 20 years.

THE LAYERS OF THE FOREST

Each of the four main layers of a South American rainforest has its own selection of plants and animals.

WHAT THEY SAY

"Perhaps we should try to emulate [copy] the North American Indian communities that have always planned many of their actions concerning the use of Nature … by giving thought to the effect they will have on the seventh unborn generation. What a difference it would make if we … thought [about] the effect our actions will have on the welfare of our great, great, great, great, great grandchildren!"
Prince Charles in his lecture at the Royal Botanic Gardens, Kew, England.

The understorey is dim and humid (warm and moist). Vines and creepers trail among the branches, orchids grow in tiny pockets of soil trapped in the forks of branches, and snakes slither in search of food.

The forest floor is surprisingly clear, except at the forest edge or near a fallen tree, where the Sun shines in. Pigs and birds grub about in the soil.

Larger animals such as tapirs and small cats live in the shrub layer.

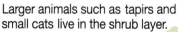

For many thousands of years, people made a living in the rainforests by "slash-and-burn" agriculture. They cut down a small patch of trees, used the wood for building or tools, burned the plants, and planted crops. This was not a problem when there were fewer people. The ash from the burnt trees fertilized the soil, giving it nutrients. Crops could be grown for a few years, and then the people would move on. The forest grew in from the edges, the soil was refreshed, and the area recovered.

In this way, much of the rainforests in Asia and Africa may have been through cycles of burning and growing over the centuries. The problem today is that there are too many people trying to live in the rainforests. This has worsened in the past 20 years. Large-scale burning has destroyed huge tracts of forest, and the trees have been replaced by grasses to feed grazing cattle (see page 27).

The canopy is bathed in sunlight. Birds, insects and monkeys feed among the fruits, flowers and leaves. There are no distinct seasons, so the animals move from one tree to another as each flowers and produces fruit. Here and there, an even taller tree (an emergent) towers more than 50 metres above the ground.

THE GREENHOUSE EFFECT

The Sun's rays pass down through the atmosphere, the blanket of air around the Earth, and warm the surface of the planet. The surface – land and sea alike – throws some of the heat back towards space. However, much of that heat does not escape into space. It is trapped by gases called greenhouse gases in the atmosphere. The main gases are carbon dioxide, CFCs (chlorofluorocarbons), methane and nitrogen oxides.

The greenhouse effect is a natural process. Without a greenhouse effect, the Earth would be 33°C cooler than it is today, and much of the planet would be

DISAPPEARING COUNTRIES?

In 1989, the deputy prime minister of Holland told the president of Brazil that if tropical forest burning continued in the Amazon until all the forest was gone, Holland would disappear. The rise in temperature due to the greenhouse effect would melt the polar ice caps and make the sea water expand. Sea levels would rise, and low-lying countries such as Holland would be flooded.

THE GREENHOUSE THREATS

BURNING FORESTS
Burning forests contribute to two major greenhouse problems. The burning wood releases carbon dioxide which adds to the greenhouse gases increasing the greenhouse effect. Also, as the forests are lost, they remove less carbon dioxide from the air by the process of **photosynthesis** (see page 36). This adds to the build-up of carbon dioxide in the atmosphere.

SHRINKING RIVERS
Water supplies in some regions would be threatened as rivers dry up, and salt seeping into the ground as sea levels rise would ruin farmland. Water is vital not just for drinking, but for many other human activities, and for industry.

frozen. Life as we know it could not exist. Most of the natural greenhouse gas is carbon dioxide, which was made originally by volcanoes. People have been putting more and more greenhouse gases into the atmosphere, especially in the past hundred years. This artificial greenhouse effect will slowly cause our world to become warmer. Many scientists now believe that, if we carry on as we are, the atmosphere will overheat disastrously in the next century. This could cause glaciers and ice sheets to melt, leading to severe flooding of low-lying lands. In other areas storms and drought could increase.

More than half of the greenhouse effect comes from carbon dioxide. About half of this carbon dioxide is produced by burning **fossil fuels** such as coal, oil and gas, as we heat our homes and drive our cars. As much as two-fifths of the carbon dioxide comes from the burning of tropical rainforests. So tropical deforestation leads to about 20 per cent of the greenhouse effect. This is a very serious problem.

FLOODED COASTLINES

World coastal regions would be under threat. As sea levels rise, coastal areas will flood, including many of the major city ports. More than one-third of the world's people live within 60 kilometres of the coast.

PARCHED FIELDS

World food production would be threatened as a result of droughts, the spread of pests, and less fresh water for irrigation. Hundreds of millions of people will die in the countries already suffering from famine. The developed countries will also start to suffer.

DEFORESTATION

THE BIG BURN-UP
Destruction does not continue all year round. In the Amazon region, and the cloud forest of Ecuador shown here, burning trees to clear the land can only be done in the dry season. Then, the skies are darkened by smoke, people suffer from breathing problems, and airports may even be closed because of poor visibility.

A common estimate for the area of rainforest destroyed each year is 200,000 square kilometres. That means an area equal to almost 40 soccer pitches every minute. The exact area is not known but estimates range between 50,000 and 420,000 square kilometres.

We could know this figure more accurately. Satellites in space send photographs back to Earth, which would allow us to see how much rainforest is disappearing. So far, they have only been used for small, local studies. A senior scientist at NASA, the US space organization, worked out that it would only cost £3 million to keep a watch on rainforest destruction. In comparison, the USA and the USSR spend at least £3,000 million each on spy satellites that take pictures of each other's weapons.

FOREST CLEARANCE
Much of the Amazon rainforest is being cleared to provide pasture for livestock or to grow crops. Huge highways are being built to allow access to the interior of the forest, which is now being felled.

LOSS OF FORESTS – THE FACTS

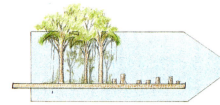

By 1980, about half of the tropical forests that had existed before people started to destroy it had gone. Only 8,000,000 square kilometres remain.

Central America has lost almost two-thirds of its rainforests to cattle ranching in the last 30 years. The cattle is sold for beefburger meat.

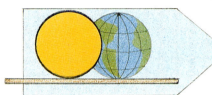

More than half of the carbon dioxide (a greenhouse gas) released by tropical forest burning comes from just six countries: Brazil, Indonesia, the Ivory Coast, Colombia, Thailand and Laos.

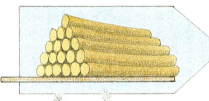

Commercial logging (the chopping down of trees such as teak and mahogany for timber) destroys around 45,000 square kilometres of tropical forests each year.

There may be 250 million small-scale farmers around the world. They destroy about 50,000 square kilometres of tropical forests each year.

Cattle ranchers burn down about 25,000 square kilometres of rainforest each year in Central America and the Amazon region of Brazil. They raise cattle to supply beefburger meat, or they lay claim to the land in case it becomes valuable in the future. In Brazil, there are valuable minerals beneath the rainforests.

Some scientists say that, at present rates of destruction, we may have lost all of our tropical rainforests by the year 2050. Much depends on how many roads are built, opening up the rainforests and allowing people to work in the interior. It also depends on the action taken by governments to stop the deforestation.

THE WATER CYCLE

MOVING WATER

Water moves around the world. It forms clouds in the atmosphere, falls to the surface as rain, drains into rivers, flows to the sea, and evaporates back into the air. From an aircraft, you can see clouds forming just above the treetops, from the water vapour given off by the forest. A nearby river has no clouds above it. In due course, the water falls down from the clouds again, as rain.

The rainforests play a vital role in natural cycles, such as the **water cycle**. This cycle is a delicate balance between the water in the soil, the trees, the rivers and the atmosphere. Many scientists believe the balance in the rainforests has a direct effect on the **weather** – and perhaps on the world's long-term climate.

Rainforests are usually centred around large river systems, which carry away the left-over water. The amount of rain that falls over the Amazon region each year is staggering: 12,000 cubic kilometres. Yet only about half of it reaches the rivers. The rest falls into the soil, and on to the leaves of the plants. The plants take up water from the soil through their roots, and release it through their leaves back into the air, as invisible water vapour. This process is called **transpiration**. Water also **evaporates** into the air directly from the soil and leaves. So great quantities of water pass into the atmosphere above the trees. There it forms clouds.

If the trees are cut down, three things happen. More rain and surface water flows into the rivers. The tree

water evaporates from trees, rivers and lakes

water condenses and falls as rain

as the air cools,
water condenses
and falls as rain,
snow or hail over
the land and sea

roots no longer bind the soil together, so soil particles are washed away too. There is also less moisture in the atmosphere to form clouds.

The extra water in the rivers causes flooding on a massive scale. Whole towns are washed away. As the problem worsens, the flood levels rise year by year. The washed-away soil clogs the streams and rivers and harms their plants and animals. When it reaches the sea, the muddy water smothers coral and sea-bed life.

More dangerous in the long term is the lack of water for clouds. The result could be less rain over the forest, a longer dry season, and a colder winter because there are no clouds to hold in the warmth. If this happens, it will spell disaster for the forest and for its people. Frosts in winter could make it difficult to grow coffee, sugar, oranges and bananas. Once under way, such a change in rainfall patterns could escalate. Computers predict that the world's climate pattern could change dramatically, affecting regions far away from the tropical forests.

water evaporates from lakes and vegetation

the rain water flows into rivers or lakes

rain water soaks into the soil, where it is used by plants or flows back to the sea

PEOPLE OF THE FORESTS

Groups of people have lived simply in the rainforests, close to nature, for thousands of years. They know how to care for the soil, and over generations they have built up great knowledge about the plants and animals, and their uses as foods and medicines.

The rainforest peoples are now dying out, along with their trees. The **World Bank** reports that Brazil's Indian population was five million in 1500 – and is under 200,000 today. Groups have shrunk in the same terrible way around the world. There is one main reason: invasion of the rainforests by outsiders. Settlers have moved in over the centuries, seeking timber, rubber, minerals and farmland.

PEOPLES IN PERIL

● On the island of Borneo, the natives have opposed the logging of their forest homelands. The Penan people blockaded roads in 1987, but the government passed harsh laws designed to crush their opposition to the logging.

● The Assurini do Katinemo people live near the Xingu river, in the heart of Brazil. They were not contacted by the outside world until 1970. There are now only 36 of them left. They seem to have lost the will to survive.

FLOODS OF DESTRUCTION

LOSS OF TRIBAL LIFE
The Asuara Indians of Ecuador (shown right) have lost much of their homeland and are having to learn to live in a changing world.

RISING RIVERS
When the rainforests are cut down, the topsoil is left unprotected. During the rainy season, the soil is washed away and the muddy water pours in to streams and rivers. The rivers cannot carry the increased volume of water and burst their banks, as here in Java (see left), causing massive flooding. The effect is disastrous. People and livestock are drowned and houses and crops destroyed.

The settlers brought diseases unknown to the natives, to which they had no resistance. In 1977, half of the Yanomami group in the northern Amazon region was wiped out by a measles epidemic. In this century, at least 87 Indian groups are known to have died out in Brazil. The settlers, far from cities and government, often considered themselves outside the law. If they wanted some land, they simply murdered the Indians living there.

The forest peoples are also at risk because of the actions of wealthy countries. The World Bank gave an enormous grant to the government of Brazil to build five huge dams on the Xingu river. This flooded the lands of several Indian groups, including the Assurini. Another group, the Kayapo, did not give up their homelands, however. They organized a meeting of thousands of their leaders, and began a protest campaign. The rock star Sting travelled to Brazil, to lend his support and bring world publicity to the Indians. In 1988 the Kayapo chief, Payakan, flew to the American capital of Washington DC and demanded that the World Bank stopped its loan. He was successful.

THE NEWCOMERS

Some people make a living in the rainforest by tapping the rubber trees. Rubber has hundreds of uses, from car tyres to pencil erasers, and it is probably the most famous commercial product of the forests. It does not harm the trees, since the tapping involves just a small slit in the bark, where the rubbery sap oozes out. The rubber tappers take care of their trees – otherwise they will lose their livelihood.

Rainforest plants also provide other products which are useful, and which can be sold. These include fibres for cloth and ropes, rubbery latex, oils, waxes, soaps, gums, resins and dyes. People who harvest and sell these products, which come from living trees, can earn their wages and support their families, provided they can use a large enough area of the forest within reach of their homes. Using the forests in this way does not harm the environment. It can best be done where the land is protected in so-called **extractive reserves**.

LONG-DISTANCE DESTRUCTION

In Central America, the number of beef cattle has increased by two-thirds in the last 20 years. In recent years, up to nine-tenths of the meat went to the USA. The American fast-food industry has probably been to blame for the destruction of more than one-quarter of the lost forests in Central America. Everyone who eats a hamburger made in this way shares the responsibility.

RUBBER TAPPING
Many rubber tappers use traditional methods to tap the rubber from the trees.

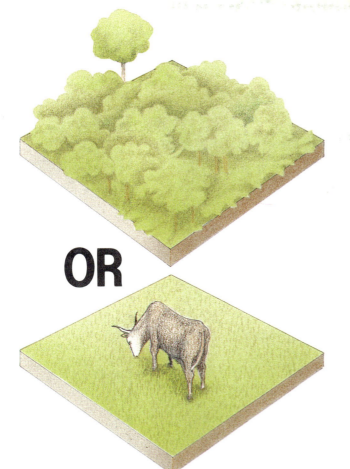

OR

=

TREES TO MEAT
It takes 5 square metres of rainforest soil (about the area covered by a small family car) to grow enough grass, to feed enough of a cow, to make the meat for one hamburger.

In the same area of undisturbed forest, there might be one large tree 20 metres tall, and up to 50 smaller trees and bushes and plants, from maybe 25 species, some of which could be very rare.

However, the rubber tappers are often not left to live and work in peace. Ranchers use the forest for cattle pasture. First, they need to burn down the trees, then they bring in the cattle, to be fattened and sold, often for hamburger meat. This business makes a lot of money for the ranchers but ravages the environment. The soil is so poor that it takes huge areas to graze the cattle. The grass that the cows eat lasts 10 years at the most. Then the ranchers have to go elsewhere and start all over again.

In Brazil, there is conflict between the cattle ranchers and the rubber tappers. Both have to work near roads. Both need large areas of forest. Their conflict has been deadly. Gunmen from private armies hired by the ranchers have murdered several leaders of the rubber tappers. On 22 December 1988, Chico Mendes was gunned down in Brazil. A rubber tapper and defender of the forests, he had been the winner of a United Nations *Global 500* award in 1987, for his work in trying to stop deforestation in his homeland.

CATTLE RANCHING
A cattle ranch on the edge of the Amazon in Bolivia.

27

BUSINESS INTERESTS

Logging companies are busy all over the world sawing down the rainforests. Most of their wood products go to Japan and Western Europe, where people like to have furniture made of hardwoods such as teak and mahogany. About 20 million cubic metres, two-fifths of all tropical rainforest hardwoods exported by these countries, goes to Japan – a country with one-fiftieth of the world's population. Much of it is used to make disposable wooden chopsticks.

About one-third of the wood exported from rain-forests is used for making paper. The average person in the industrialized countries uses 150 kilograms of paper each year, equivalent to the weight of three adult people. Most of this is unnecessary. The developed countries could save huge amounts of paper by recycling. They could grow most, if not all, of the wood they need in their own forests.

WOOD PRODUCTION FOR PAPER

Country	Increase since 1974-76
Africa	84%
South America	81%
Asia	71%
Europe	32%
Oceania	31%
North and Central America	27%
USSR	16%

LOGGING
In Nigeria many rubber trees are being cut down and the forest cleared for other uses.

Wood is by no means the only **resource** that attracts big business to the rainforests. There are huge deposits of minerals below the ground. In Brazil, the Greater Carajas Project wants to mine gold, copper and other minerals from nearly 1,000,000 square kilometres of rainforest. Poorly-paid miners struggle through seas of mud each day, looking for gold. They use mercury to separate the gold from the mud. This dangerous substance harms their bodies and poisons the rivers.

LAND EROSION
Gold prospecting has caused massive erosion of the land and loss of the topsoil in the Pantanal region of Brazil.

ANNUAL WOOD PRODUCTION

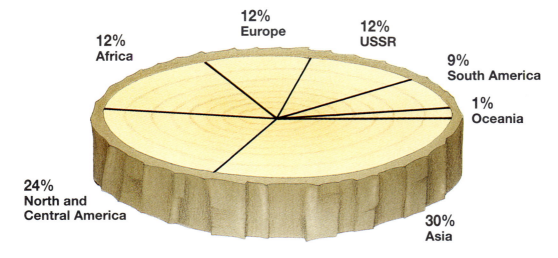

12%
Europe

12%
Africa

12%
USSR

9%
South America

1%
Oceania

24%
North and
Central America

30%
Asia

World production = 7000 million cubic metres (100%)

MEDICINE, FOOD, FUEL

winged bean

hyacinth bean

CROP OF THE FUTURE?
You can eat any part of the winged bean of New Guinea – roots, stem, leaves, seeds and flowers. A drink like coffee can be made from its juice. This plant grows quickly, to a height of 5 metres, and is just as nutritious as soybeans. Rainforests could be full of similar useful plants.

The pods of the hyacinth bean can be eaten in a variety of ways. It is grown widely in India and Africa.

Many of our most vital medicines are based on chemicals from rainforest plants. We use these chemicals in antibiotics which fight infections, and in drugs that treat heart disease, ulcers, depression and many other illnesses. Plants from the rainforests also contain chemicals that may help to fight cancer. Of the 3000 plants which help treat cancer that have been identified by the US National Cancer Institute, over two-thirds come from the rainforests. The business based on drugs derived from rainforest plants is worth millions of pounds each year.

We use fewer than one in 1000 plant species for food. In this sense, we are very unadventurous. In the earliest days of farming, over 10,000 years ago, our ancestors changed their hunting-and-gathering lifestyle and started to settle down to grow the first crops. They rapidly discovered that about 20 species were good to eat. These plants, such as wheat, rye, millet and rice, have been our staple foods ever since. Yet we know that at least 75,000 plant species have edible parts. In the rainforests, at least 1650 plants could become vegetable crops.

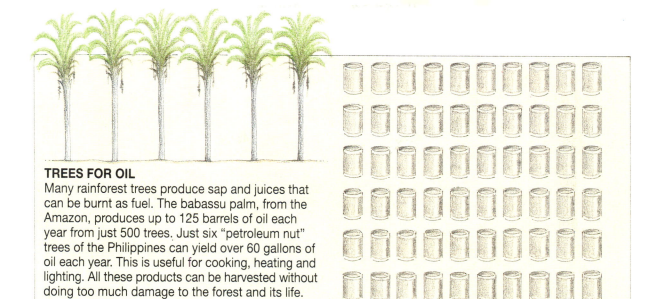

TREES FOR OIL

Many rainforest trees produce sap and juices that can be burnt as fuel. The babassu palm, from the Amazon, produces up to 125 barrels of oil each year from just 500 trees. Just six "petroleum nut" trees of the Philippines can yield over 60 gallons of oil each year. This is useful for cooking, heating and lighting. All these products can be harvested without doing too much damage to the forest and its life.

FIGHTING LEUKAEMIA IN CHILDREN

A rainforest plant from Madagascar, the rosy periwinkle, contains chemicals that have been dramatically successful in fighting leukaemia (a type of blood cancer) in children. Leukaemia is a deadly disease which only one-fifth of affected children used to survive before drug treatment. With this drug treatment, almost nine-tenths now survive.

THE DEBT CRISIS

Part of the problem of tropical deforestation is that the undeveloped countries, and especially those that have rainforests, owe a great deal of money to the developed countries. These countries may have few resources. Even if they have valuable minerals or precious metals, they lack the money to mine and extract them. Chopping down trees and selling the timber is seen as an easy way to pay the debts.

The problem began in the 1970s. Around that time some 550 private banks in Europe, North America and Japan, loaned hundreds of billions of dollars to the developing countries. Many governments also made big loans. The total amount of money lent during this period was about £500 billion. About two-thirds came from the banks, and the rest from governments. For comparison, the whole world spends about the same amount on weapons each year. We can also compare these debts with the money made by the world's richest companies. The 200 top companies made about £1,500 billion in 1984. Many companies are richer than whole countries.

The loans were far from free. The less-developed countries had to pay back the loan itself, and also interest on top. Some countries are so heavily in debt that they have trouble just paying the extra money, or interest for borrowing the money. The total repayments for the interest alone amounts to about £20 billion each year. Many countries owe more on the loan and the interest than they could ever make by selling their resources and goods, such as coffee, copper or timber.

The result of such an impossible situation is that there is less and less money for governments to spend on their people. The standard of living falls. Poor people become too busy just trying to survive from one day to the next, to spend time worrying about the rainforests. If this situation continues, can we ever expect to see an end to the destruction of the rainforests in the developing countries?

MOUNTING DEBTS

Brazil is the main rainforest country, and it is also the main debtor country. It owes more than £50 billion now, and is getting deeper and deeper into debt. Between 1982 and 1987, Brazil paid back £35 billion in loan and interest repayments to governments and the private banks of developed countries. Yet it was £10 billion deeper in debt in 1987 than in 1982.

WHAT THEY SAY

"The simple, and terrible, truth is that poverty and environment are … linked in a chain of cause and effect. Problems of [the] environment cannot be tackled in isolation from those national and international economic factors that perpetuate [continue indefinitely] large scale poverty."
Shridath Rampahal, Commonwealth Secretary General, February 1989.

"THIRD WORLD" DEBTS

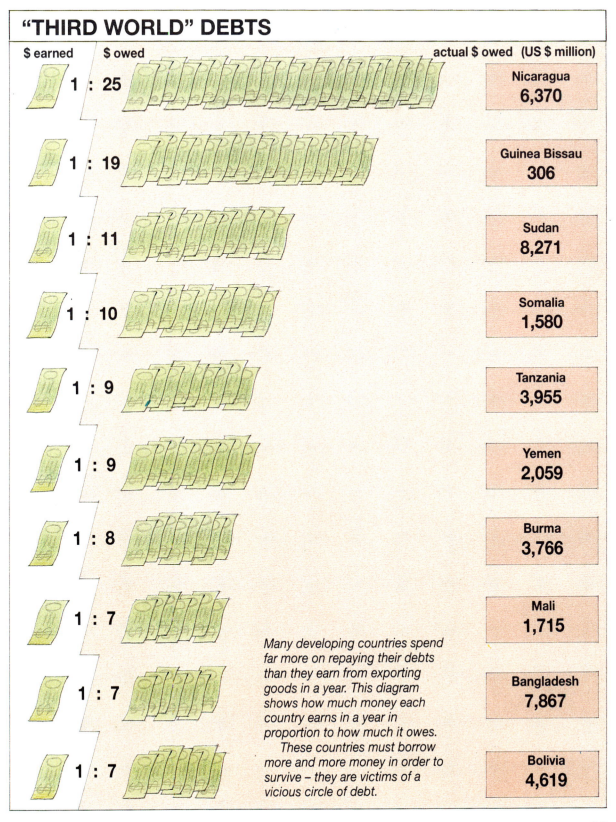

$ earned	$ owed	actual $ owed (US $ million)
1 : 25		**Nicaragua** 6,370
1 : 19		**Guinea Bissau** 306
1 : 11		**Sudan** 8,271
1 : 10		**Somalia** 1,580
1 : 9		**Tanzania** 3,955
1 : 9		**Yemen** 2,059
1 : 8		**Burma** 3,766
1 : 7		**Mali** 1,715
1 : 7		**Bangladesh** 7,867
1 : 7		**Bolivia** 4,619

Many developing countries spend far more on repaying their debts than they earn from exporting goods in a year. This diagram shows how much money each country earns in a year in proportion to how much it owes.

These countries must borrow more and more money in order to survive – they are victims of a vicious circle of debt.

RISK FACTORS

TROPICAL TREASURE TROVE

Tropical forests contain at least 50% of all known species. Present information suggests that rainforests contain, for example, 80% of insects; 90% of primates; 90% of ferns; 65% of mosses.

Can we really go on cutting down our forests so fast? Can we afford to ignore the warning signs? If we carry on, think of the way we would be adding to global warming. Up to one-fifth of the greenhouse effect is due to carbon dioxide produced by burning the forests. Suppose we go on adding this and other greenhouse gases to the air at the rate we do today. If scientists are right with their computer forecasts, then we will have to face rates of temperature rise that are 10 to 100 times faster than Nature has known for hundreds of thousands of years.

Think of the other risks we are taking with the climate. We have seen how the process of cloud formation above the tropical rainforests is vital to their well-being. We know that if we reduce the number of clouds, the forests will start dying even before they can be all cut down. If all the forests go, what will be the effect on world climate patterns? No one can say, but we can be sure it will be bad.

FOREST HIGHWAYS
In the montane rainforest of Ecuador, 2000 metres above sea level, vast highways are being built to allow access for people and machinery.

Think of the medicines we may be missing. So few of the rainforest plants have been tested for their usefulness as medicines. Those that have are often life-savers. Even now, a plant capable of curing cancer may be going into extinction under a bulldozer or in fire. It is a depressing thought.

Think of the foods we have not tried. In the future, we will be struggling to feed all our people, even without problems such as the greenhouse effect. With hundreds of tropical rainforest plants that could be good vegetable crops, and thousands yet to be tested, can we continue to rely on the few crops we have today? If we allow the rainforests to disappear, we will not even have the choice.

WHAT THEY SAY

"I resent the creation of a world in which beauty is a reminder of what we are losing, rather than a celebration of what we've got."
Ben Elton, television personality and comedian.

EFFECTS OF FOREST DESTRUCTION

Scientists admit they may be wrong – it could be worse. Several factors might make the temperature rise even faster.

The oceans might soak up less carbon dioxide in a warming world than they do today, so there would be more left in the air to increase the greenhouse effect.

Melting ice could mean that less of the Sun's heat is reflected back into space. This would mean more heat would be absorbed by the ground and reflected upwards, to be trapped in the atmosphere by greenhouse gases.

Warming soils could release more carbon dioxide into the atmosphere. Again, the air temperature would be pushed up. Within a few years we could be seeing untold extra misery in the world. There will be devastation in the rainforests and other natural places, as the plants and animals fail to cope with the increasing temperatures and die out as the web of life falls apart.

WE NEED MORE FORESTS

There are many reasons for stopping deforestation, but there is also a vital reason for planting more forests. It is the greenhouse effect.

At present, we are putting about 20,000 million tonnes of carbon dioxide gas into the atmosphere each year as we burn coal, oil and gas. About half of this gas is soaked up by the sea, but the rest builds up in the atmosphere. Carbon dioxide is a greenhouse gas (see page 18), and so its build-up could help overheat the Earth.

Can we help? Trees and plants can take carbon dioxide out of the atmosphere. They use it to make food in their leaves, by the process of photosynthesis. So planting many new forests is one way to reduce the amount of greenhouse gas in the atmosphere. This would reduce the many dangers which the greenhouse effect poses to the natural world, and to humans.

USING UP CARBON DIOXIDE

In the process of photosynthesis, a plant takes in carbon dioxide gas from the air, and adds it to water and minerals from the soil, using the energy from sunlight. In this way, the plant makes sugars for energy, and builds up its own body as it grows. So photosynthesis converts carbon dioxide into living plant matter, which animals can use for food.

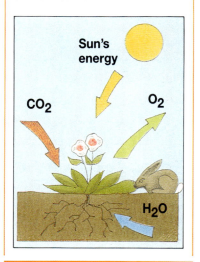

TREE PLANTING
In some areas, such as here in Ethiopia, trees are being planted in an effort to restore the natural forest habitats.

How much new forest could we plant? The choice is ours. There are massive areas of land in the tropics where forests once stood. The trees could be replanted. In the developed countries, where most of the natural forests were cut down more than a century ago, there is also plenty of land which could be reforested.

Many farms in the developed countries now produce food which adds to the surplus **"food mountains"**. Some of the farmers could be encouraged to turn into foresters. Also, we might change our ways of using the timber. For example, if we recycled more paper, we would need to cut down fewer trees. The animals and plants that are slowly being killed off would have new places to live. So planting new forests can help. We also need other ways of dealing with the greenhouse effect, as explained on the next page.

HOW MUCH FOREST?

Suppose we wanted to take out of the atmosphere all the carbon dioxide from the burning of coal, oil and gas. We would need to plant an area of forest almost as big as Australia! This cannot be done in a short time. Creating more forests, instead of destroying them, would greatly help to slow down the greenhouse effect. Areas of forest that have been cut down in the past (see below) are being replanted as forest plantations.

SOLVING THE PROBLEMS

The greenhouse effect threatens all the natural world, including forests. Even if we act now, it is likely to get much worse in the coming years before it gets better. Biologists say that many trees and animals will not be able to adapt to the higher temperatures, and they will die out. Stopping tropical deforestation is an important part of our efforts to tackle the greenhouse effect.

WHAT CAN WE DO?

TREES OR WEAPONS?

International effort is needed to stop tropical deforestation. The world spends millions of pounds each day on weapons. The former energy minister of Brazil calculated that about £2,000 million would save two-thirds of the Amazon rainforests – the same amount of money that the USA plans to spend on just six of its new B-2 "Stealth" bombers.

Improve public transport, and use it more often. People should be able to travel without having to use cars all the time.

Reduce the carbon dioxide gas that is being released into the atmosphere. Most of it comes from burning coal in power stations, and burning oil and petrol in cars and trucks.

Persuade people and industries to cut down on greenhouse gases. Governments could make laws and give grants that encourage anti-greenhouse ways of life. They could also put extra taxes on the wasteful use of coal, oil and gas.

Help the developing countries. If the total amounts of greenhouse gases are to be cut, these countries need aid in the form of money, modern technology and advice. Then they will not need to pursue the wasteful uses of energy, which the developed countries did while they were building up their industrial societies in the past.

WE NEED RAINFORESTS

Rainforests store massive amounts of carbon in the living vegetation. When this is released by burning or as they decay, the amount of carbon dioxide in the air increases. Once destroyed, the trees no longer take up the carbon dioxide needed for photosynthesis. The balance of carbon dioxide production and uptake is destroyed.

Use energy more efficiently. We can build well-insulated houses to save heat energy, and use machines that use less electricity or fuel energy.

Use renewable forms of energy. We must make more electricity and heat from forms of energy, such as solar power, wind power and wave power, which will not run out – and which produce hardly any carbon dioxide.

Improve research and monitoring of the environment. There are many uncertainties about how bad the greenhouse effect will be. Scientists need to understand more about how Nature works, so that governments can see that there is a need for action.

Invest huge amounts of money in fighting the greenhouse effect. All countries must act if we are to avoid disaster. Such investment will cost billions of pounds. We could have enough money – but it is currently spent on other things. The world's weapons cost billions of pounds each year. We will have to decide which is the bigger threat: war or a global climate disaster.

SAVE THE FORESTS

How can we save the forests of the world, and especially the tropical rainforests?

Some people say that we must allow people to cut down the trees, but in a controlled and sensible way. New trees would be planted to grow at the same rate as old ones are cut down. Logging would happen in selected places, so that the animals had time to move and adapt. Supporters of this approach say that it is better than simply stopping the timber trade. They argue that if logging is banned, the people who relied on it for a living would be out of work. They might start to burn the forests and use the land for agriculture.

Other people disagree. They say that controlled logging is still an invasion of lands where forest people have lived for centuries, and that you cannot be sure

THE "DEBT-FOR-NATURE" SWAP

One suggestion for saving the rainforests is that the developed countries should allow part or all of the huge debt that less-developed countries owe them to be spent on helping the forests. This idea is called the "debt-for-nature" swap.

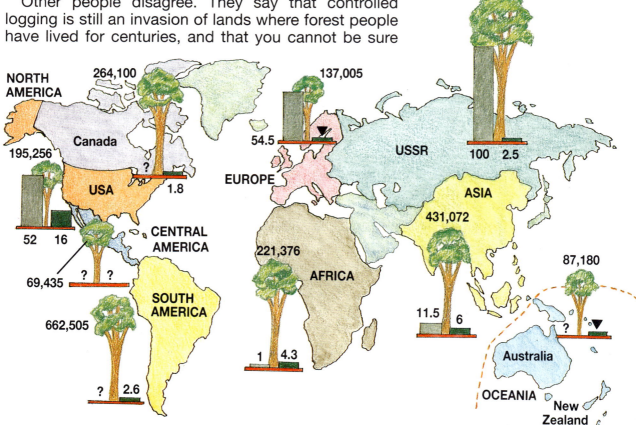

FAMOUS NATURAL SANCTUARY

One famous example of a protected rainforest is the beautiful Korup National Park, in Cameroon, Africa (see right). A huge area is cared for in its natural state. The local people make money from tourists and scientific organizations which study the forest in detail.

PROTECTED FORESTS

From the few figures available, it appears that less than 4% of the world's tropical rainforest is officially protected (see the map on the left) in 600 separate sites. Costa Rica, a small country in Central America, now has national parks covering about 10% of its area. Only about 3% of the world's rainforests are under good management, where trees are planted as fast as they are cut down.

The situation for some coniferous and temperate forests is no better. Few forests are protected, although many are now officially managed.

KEY

 Closed forest (forests, not shrubland or open woodland; thousand hectares)

Managed forest %

 Protected forest %

?   **value unknown**

▼   **less than 1%**

of balancing deforestation with planting new trees. In most tropical countries, only one tree is planted for every 10 that are cut down. They argue that the only choice is to halt the destruction altogether, and turn the forests into great parks where people can only make their living in ways that do not harm the wildlife.

Scientists have shown that the second approach makes more sense. In a typical area of forest, people can make money by harvesting products like fruit and rubber from the trees, and by selling things like medicinal plants gathered from below the trees – all without destroying the forest. This is the use of extractive reserves (see page 26). In the long term it would earn more than destroying the area by cutting timber or raising cattle.

WHAT YOU CAN DO

There are many ways that we can all help if we are worried about the disappearing forests and other environmental problems. Trees are being destroyed for many reasons. They are being felled to provide wood for fuel and furniture; they are being burnt down to make more room for crops and cattle; they are being killed by acid rain produced by the gases given off by cars, trucks, power stations and factories. There are many steps that we can all take to help in each of these areas.

CONSUMER POWER

● Buy goods locally

● Don't buy beefburgers at fast-food restaurants that use beef produced on tropical rainforest ranches

● Write to leaders of industry explaining the importance of saving rainforests

● Write to your local government representative or to world leaders about the loss of the world's forests

ENERGY

● Insulate your home so that you use less fuel to keep it warm

● Turn down the thermostat in your home or office by a few degrees. You will hardly notice the difference, but it will save a lot of energy

● Turn off lights or other electrical equipment when not in use. Use energy-efficient light bulbs

● Turn the thermostat on the hot water heater down a few degrees. Turn off the hot water heater when it is not in use

TRANSPORT

● Cars are one of the biggest polluters in the world. Cut down on the fumes produced by using a catalytic converter on your car

● Use lead-free petrol if possible

● Choose a fuel-efficient, low-polluting car

● Use public transport whenever possible

● Share your car on trips to school and work

TREES

● Ask your parents not to buy products made out of tropical rainforest wood – rosewood, teak, ebony and mahogany – unless it as the "Good Wood" seal of approval and is made from trees grown on special plantations

● Avoid using disposable paper products. It takes one 15-year-old tree to make about 700 large paper bags. Say "No" to extra paper bags

● Plant a tree – if 100,000 people each planted a tree this year, the trees would be taking in over 400 tonnes of carbon dioxide every year within 20 years

● Collect waste paper to be used in recycling

● Try and buy goods made from recycled paper

BUSINESS

● Use low-polluting,energy-efficient fleet cars

● Do not buy or import tropical hardwoods felled from rainforests

● Do not import beef raised on tropical forest ranches

● Do not invest in mining in tropical forest areas

● Invest in businesses in the developing countries that do not destroy forests

GOVERNMENT

● Organize and finance the planting of trees, especially broad-leaved woodland trees

● Pass measures encouraging people and industries to adopt anti-greenhouse ways.

● Support organizations that are involved in conserving rainforests

● Encourage and develop plans to use renewable energy sources

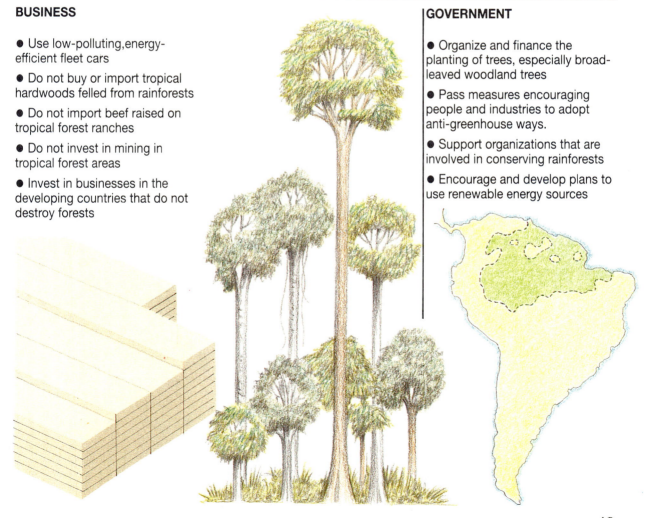

GLOSSARY

Acid rain   Rain, dew, or snow which is more acidic than is natural. Acid rain is produced by the sulphur dioxide and nitrogen oxides which are given off when fossil fuels are burned.

Climate   The weather conditions typically experienced in an area over periods of years.

Deforestation   The cutting down or burning of forests to clear them of trees. The trees are often used as timber if they are cut down – this is called logging.

Evaporation   Water lost to the air as water vapour.

Evolution   The gradual changes of plants and animals over time. A group of individuals in one species of living thing can change so much over time – especially if they are isolated from other groups of individuals – that a new species forms.

Extinct   When the last member of a species dies, that species has become extinct. Many dinosaur species became extinct all at once 66 million years ago. Species that are in danger of becoming extinct are "endangered" species. There are many endangered species living in tropical rainforests.

Extractive reserves   An area of forest reserved only for people to make a living in ways that do not involve damaging the trees. For example, the withdrawal of rubber sap from trees without killing the trees and the picking of Brazil nuts.

Food mountains   These are surpluses of food which build up when agriculture is subsidised by governments or when farms produce too much for local needs.

Fossil fuels   Fossil fuels are coal, oil, and gas. They are all made of carbon, and if you burn them you get carbon dioxide – a greenhouse gas – and the gases that produce acid rain.

Nutrients   The chemicals and minerals, such as phosphates and nitrates, that are taken up by the roots of plants.

Resource   A resource is something that humans find useful. A natural resource can be defined in various ways. For some people, coal is a natural resource: you can burn it to make energy. For other people, coal should not be viewed as a natural resource, because when you burn it you get greenhouse gases and acid rain. Also, there are other ways to make energy that do not harm the environment so much. To some people the tropical rainforests are not themselves a natural resource: the forests are only in the way of getting at other natural resources such as gold. To other people, the tropical rainforests are very much themselves a natural resource – they are like the "lungs" of the planet, and without them the world would be hotter, drier and less able to support its human population.

Photosynthesis   The process by which green plants make food from carbon dioxide gas and water using the energy of the Sun.

Transpiration   The passage of water up through a plant. Water is drawn in by the roots and evaporated from the leaves.

Water cycle   The routes which water follows from one part of the environment to another. For example, water can go from the sea to the air as a result of evaporation on a hot day. It can form clouds in the air and later fall on land, drain into a river and find its way back into the sea.

Weather   The conditions of temperature, rainfall and wind experienced by an area on a day-to-day basis.

World Bank   An international bank set up by the United Nations which lends money to governments to try to help them build up their economies.

FURTHER READING

For Children

Forests by Terry Jennings; Oxford University Press, 1986.

Disappearing Rainforests by Robert Presser; Batsford Educational, 1988.

What is a Rain Forest? by Philip Whitfield; British Museum of Natural History, 1989.

Conserving the Jungles by Laurence Williams; Evans, 1989.

Conserving Rainforests by Martin Banks; Wayland, 1989.

Trees of the Tropics by Jennifer Cochrane; Heinemann, 1990.

Fir Trees by Theresa Greenaway; Heinemann, 1990.

For Adults

Jungles by Edward Ayenson (editor); Jonathon Cape, 1980.

The Primary Source by Norman Myers; Norton, 1984.

Green Inheritance by A. Huxley; Collins, 1984.

In the Rainforest by Catherine Caufield; Picador, 1984.

Plant and Planet by A. Huxley; Collins, 1987.

Saving the Tropical Forests by J. Gradwohl and R. Greenberg; Earthscan Publications, 1988.

USEFUL ADDRESSES

Department of the Environment (DoE)
2, Marsham Street, London SW1
The DoE has many leaflets and guidelines on environmental issues.

Council for Environmental Education
School of Education, University of Reading, London Road, Reading, Berks RG1 5AQ
Helps youth organizations to learn more about the environment.

Friends of the Earth (FoE)
26–28 Underwood Street, London N1
FoE is an action group that organizes campaigns on environmental issues. They have a youth section, Earth Action, for people aged 14 to 23.

Greenpeace UK
30–31 Islington Green, London N1 8XE
Greenpeace organizes protests and campaigns against the destruction of the environment. They also present scientific information on various environmental projects to many governments. They will answer questions and give advice to organizations and schoolchildren who write to them.

Waste Watch
National Council for Voluntary Organizations, 26 Bedford Square, London WC1B 3HU.
Details of local environmental groups and voluntary organizations in the UK are available from Waste Watch.

WATCH Trust for Environmental Education Ltd
22 The Green, Nettleham, Lincoln LN2 2NR
WATCH works with schools and helps to organize conservation projects. It aims to increase knowledge of the natural world and encourage conservation.

Woodland Trust
Autumn Park, Grantham, Lincolnshire NG31 6LL
The Woodland Trust helps to maintain forests and woodlands. It sometimes buys woodland that is endangered.

World Wide Fund for Nature (WWF)
Panda House, Weyside Park, Godalming, Surrey GU7 1XR
WWF encourages the conservation of plants and animals throughout the world.

INDEX